MznLnx

Missing Links Exam Preps

Exam Prep for

Trigonometry

Baley, Sarell, 3rd Edition

The MznLnx Exam Prep is your link from the texbook and lecture to your exams.
The MznLnx Exam Preps are unauthorized and comprehensive reviews of your textbooks.

All material provided by MznLnx and Rico Publications (c) 2010
Textbook publishers and textbook authors do not particpate in or contribute to these reviews.

MznLnx

Rico
Publications

Exam Prep for Trigonometry
3rd Edition
Baley, Sarell

Publisher: Raymond Houge
Assistant Editor: Michael Rouger
Text and Cover Designer: Lisa Buckner
Marketing Manager: Sara Swagger
Project Manager, Editorial Production: Jerry Emerson
Art Director: Vernon Lowerui

Product Manager: Dave Mason
Editorial Assitant: Rachel Guzmanji
Pedagogy: Debra Long
Cover Image: Jim Reed/Getty Images
Text and Cover Printer: City Printing, Inc.
Compositor: Media Mix, Inc.

(c) 2010 Rico Publications
ALL RIGHTS RESERVED. No part of this work
covered by the copyright may be reproduced or
used in any form or by an means--graphic, electronic,
or mechanical, including photocopying, recording,
taping, Web distribution, information storage, and
retrieval systems, or in any other manner--without the
written permission of the publisher.

Printed in the United States
ISBN:

> For more information about our products, contact us at:
> Dave.Mason@RicoPublications.com
>
> For permission to use material from this text or
> product, submit a request online to:
> Dave.Mason@RicoPublications.com

Contents

CHAPTER 1
Measurement of Angles, Arcs, and Sectors 1

CHAPTER 2
The Trigonometric Functions 8

CHAPTER 3
Graphs of the Trigonometric Functions 17

CHAPTER 4
Inverse Trigonometric Functions 22

CHAPTER 5
Basic Trigonometric Identities 27

CHAPTER 6
Sum and Difference Identities 30

CHAPTER 7
Additional Identities 32

CHAPTER 8
Trigonometric Equations 33

CHAPTER 9
Law of Sines and Law of Cosines 35

CHAPTER 10
Vectors 39

CHAPTER 11
Complex Numbers 43

CHAPTER 12
Polar Coordinates 46

ANSWER KEY 49

TO THE STUDENT

COMPREHENSIVE

The *MznLnx* Exam Prep series is designed to help you pass your exams. Editors at MznLnx review your textbooks and then prepare these practice exams to help you master the textbook material. Unlike study guides, workbooks, and practice tests provided by the texbook publisher and textbook authors, *MznLnx* gives you **all** of the material in each chapter in exam form, not just samples, so you can be sure to nail your exam.

MECHANICAL

The MznLnx Exam Prep series creates exams that will help you learn the subject matter as well as test you on your understanding. Each question is designed to help you master the concept. Just working through the exams, you gain an understanding of the subject--its a simple mechanical process that produces success.

INTEGRATED STUDY GUIDE AND REVIEW

MznLnx is not just a set of exams designed to test you, its also a comprehensive review of the subject content. Each exam question is also a review of the concept, making sure that you will get the answer correct without having to go to other sources of material. You learn as you go! Its the easiest way to pass an exam.

HUMOR

Studying can be tedious and dry. MznLnx's instructional design includes moderate humor within the exam questions on occassion, to break the tedium and revitalize the brain

Chapter 1. Measurement of Angles, Arcs, and Sectors

1. In geometry and trigonometry, an _____ is the figure formed by two rays sharing a common endpoint, called the vertex of the _____ . The magnitude of the _____ is the 'amount of rotation' that separates the two rays, and can be measured by considering the length of circular arc swept out when one ray is rotated about the vertex to coincide with the other Where there is no possibility of confusion, the term '_____' is used interchangeably for both the geometric configuration itself and for its angular magnitude (which is simply a numerical quantity.)
   a. Additive identity
   b. Angle
   c. Absolute value
   d. Affinely extended real number system

2. In Euclidean geometry, a _____ is a straight curve. When geometry is used to model the real world, _____s are used to represent straight objects with negligible width and height. _____s are an idealisation of such objects and have no width or height at all and are usually considered to be infinitely long.
   a. Best fit
   b. Line
   c. Belt problem
   d. Bounded

3. _____ is a part of mathematics concerned with questions of size, shape, and relative position of figures and with properties of space. _____ is one of the oldest sciences. Initially a body of practical knowledge concerning lengths, areas, and volumes, in the third century BC _____ was put into an axiomatic form by Euclid, whose treatment--Euclidean _____--set a standard for many centuries to follow.
   a. Belt problem
   b. Geometry
   c. Bounded
   d. Best fit

4. A _____ is one of the basic shapes of geometry: a polygon with three corners or vertices and three sides or edges which are line segments. A _____ with vertices A, B, and C is denoted ABC.

   In Euclidean geometry any three non-collinear points determine a unique _____ and a unique plane (i.e. a two-dimensional Euclidean space.)

   a. Best fit
   b. Triangle
   c. Bounded
   d. Belt problem

5. A _____ is a simple shape of Euclidean geometry consisting of those points in a plane which are the same distance from a given point called the centre. The common distance of the points of a _____ from its center is called its radius.

_____s are simple closed curves which divide the plane into two regions, an interior and an exterior.

   a. Bounded
   b. Circle
   c. Belt problem
   d. Best fit

6. The _____ is the distance around a closed curve. _____ is a special perimeter.

The _____ of a circle is the length around it.

   a. Belt problem
   b. Bounded
   c. Best fit
   d. Circumference

7. In geometry, a _____ of a circle is any straight line segment that passes through the center of the circle and whose endpoints are on the circle. The _____s are the longest chords of the circle. The word '_____' derives from Greek διἀμετρος , 'diagonal of a circle', from δια- (dia-), 'across, through' + μἱτρον (metron), 'a measure'.)
   a. Diameter
   b. Belt problem
   c. Bounded
   d. Best fit

8. The _____ is a unit of plane angle, equal to 180/π (or 360/2π) degrees or about 57°17′45″. It is the standard unit of angular measurement in all areas of mathematics beyond the elementary level.

The _____ is represented by the symbol 'rad' or, more rarely, by the superscript c (for 'circular measure'.)

   a. Best fit
   b. Bounded
   c. Radian
   d. Belt problem

Chapter 1. Measurement of Angles, Arcs, and Sectors 3

9. A pair of angles are complementary if the sum of their measures is 90 degrees.

If the two _____ are adjacent (i.e. have a common vertex and share just one side) their non-shared sides form a right angle.

In Euclidean geometry, the two acute angles in a right triangle are complementary, because the sum of internal angles of a triangle is 180 degrees, and the right angle itself accounts for ninety degrees.

  a. Line
  b. Belt problem
  c. Complementary angles
  d. Best fit

10. In geometry and trigonometry, a _____ is an angle of 90 degrees, corresponding to a quarter turn (that is, a quarter of a full circle.) It can be defined as the angle such that twice that angle amounts to a half turn, or 180°.

Lines that are at a _____ to each other are perpendicular, an important geometrical property.

  a. Best fit
  b. Right angle
  c. Belt problem
  d. Bounded

11. _____ are pairs of angles whose measures add up to 180 degrees. If the two _____ are adjacent (i.e. have a common vertex and share just one side), their non-shared sides form a line. The supplement of an angle of 135 degrees is an angle of 45 degrees.
  a. Best fit
  b. Supplementary angles
  c. Belt problem
  d. Bounded

12. In category theory, an abstract branch of mathematics, an _____ of a category C is an object I in C such that for every object X in C, there exists precisely one morphism I → X. The dual notion is that of a terminal object (also called terminal element): T is terminal if for every object X in C there exists a single morphism X → T. _____s are also called coterminal or universal, and terminal objects are also called final.

Chapter 1. Measurement of Angles, Arcs, and Sectors

If an object is both initial and terminal, it is called a zero object or null object.

- The empty set is the unique _____ in the category of sets; every one-element set (singleton) is a terminal object in this category; there are no zero objects.
- Similarly, the empty space is the unique _____ in the category of topological spaces; every one-point space is a terminal object in this category.
- In the category of non-empty sets, there are no _____s. The singletons are not initial: while every non-empty set admits a function from a singleton, this function is in general not unique.
- In the category of groups, any trivial group is a zero object. The same is true for the categories of abelian groups, modules over a ring, and vector spaces over a field. This is the origin of the term 'zero object'.
- In the category of semigroups, the empty semigroup is an _____ and any singleton semigroup is a terminal object. There are no zero objects. In the subcategory of monoids, however, every trivial monoid (consisting of only the identity element) is a zero object.
- In the category of pointed sets (whose objects are non-empty sets together with a distinguished element; a morphism from (A,a) to (B,b) being a function f : A → B with f(a) = b), every singleton is a zero object. Similarly, in the category of pointed topological spaces, every singleton is a zero object.
- In the category of rings with unity and unity-perserving morphisms, the ring of integers Z is an _____. The trivial ring consisting only of a single element 0=1 is a terminal object. In the category of general rings with homomorphisms, the trivial ring is a zero object.
- In the category of fields, there are no initial or terminal objects. However, in the subcategory of fields of characteristic p, the prime field of characteristic p forms an _____.
- Any partially ordered set (P, ≤) can be interpreted as a category: the objects are the elements of P, and there is a single morphism from x to y if and only if x ≤ y. This category has an _____ if and only if P has a least element; it has a terminal object if and only if P has a greatest element.
- If a monoid is considered as a category with a single object, this object is neither initial or terminal unless the monoid is trivial, in which case it is both.
- In the category of graphs, the null graph (without vertices and edges) is an _____. The graph with a single vertex and a single loop is terminal. The category of simple graphs does not have a terminal object.
- Similarly, the category of all small categories with functors as morphisms has the empty category as _____ and the category 1 (with a single object and morphism) as terminal object.
- Any topological space X can be viewed as a category by taking the open sets as objects, and a single morphism between two open sets U and V if and only if U ⊂ V. The empty set is the _____ of this category, and X is the terminal object. This is a special case of the case 'partially ordered set', mentioned above. Take P:= the set of open subsets
- If X is a topological space (viewed as a category as above) and C is some small category, we can form the category of all contravariant functors from X to C, using natural transformations as morphisms. This category is called the category of presheaves on X with values in C. If C has an _____ c, then the constant functor which sends every open set to c is an _____ in the category of presheaves. Similarly, if C has a terminal object, then the corresponding constant functor serves as a terminal presheaf.
- In the category of schemes, Spec(Z) the prime spectrum of the ring of integers is a terminal object. The empty scheme (equal to the prime spectrum of the trivial ring) is an _____.
- If we fix a homomorphism f : A → B of abelian groups, we can consider the category C consisting of all pairs (X, φ) where X is an abelian group and φ : X → A is a group homomorphism with f φ = 0. A morphism from the pair (X, φ) to the pair (Y, ψ) is defined to be a group homomorphism r : X → Y with the property ψ r = φ. The kernel of f is a terminal object in this category; this is nothing but a reformulation of the universal property of kernels. With an analogous construction, the cokernel of f can be seen as an _____ of a suitable category.
- In the category of interpretations of an algebraic model, the _____ is the initial algebra, the interpretation that provides as many distinct objects as the model allows and no more.

Chapter 1. Measurement of Angles, Arcs, and Sectors 5

Initial and terminal objects are not required to exist in a given category. However, if they do exist, they are essentially unique.

  a. Absolute value
  b. Initial object
  c. Affinely extended real number system
  d. Additive identity

13. For some curves there is a smallest number L that is an upper bound on the length of any polygonal approximation. If such a number exists, then the curve is said to be rectifiable and the curve is defined to have _____ L.

Let C be a curve in Euclidean (or, more generally, a metric) space $X = R^n$, so C is the image of a continuous function f : [a, b] → X of the interval [a, b] into X.

From a partition $a = t_0 < t_1 < ... < t_{n-1} < t_n = b$ of the interval [a, b] we obtain a finite collection of points $f(t_0)$, $f(t_1)$, ..., $f(t_{n-1})$, $f(t_n)$ on the curve C. Denote the distance from $f(t_i)$ to $f(t_{i+1})$ by $d(f(t_i), f(t_{i+1}))$, which is the length of the line segment connecting the two points.

  a. Absolute value
  b. Affinely extended real number system
  c. Additive identity
  d. Arc length

14. A _____ or circle sector, is the portion of a circle enclosed by two radii and an arc, where the smaller area is known as the minor sector and the larger being the major sector. Its area can be calculated as described below.

Let θ be the central angle, in radians, and r the radius.

  a. Bounded
  b. Circular sector
  c. Belt problem
  d. Best fit

15. Conversion of units refers to _____ between different units of measurement for the same quantity.

The process of making a conversion cannot produce a more precise result than the original quoted figure. Appropriate rounding of results is normally performed after conversion.

a. Decibel
b. Belt problem
c. Best fit
d. Conversion factors

16. A mile is a unit of length, usually used to measure distance, in a number of different systems. In contemporary English, mile most commonly refers to the _____ of 5,280 feet (exactly 1,609.344 meters) or the nautical mile of 1,852 meters (about 6,076.1 ft.) There are many other historical miles, and similar units in other systems translated as miles in English, varying between one and fifteen kilometers.
  a. Bounded
  b. Best fit
  c. Belt problem
  d. Statute mile

17. A _____ is an angle whose vertex is the center of a circle, and whose sides pass through a pair of points on the circle, thereby subtending an arc between those two points whose angle is (by definition) equal to the _____ itself. It is also known as the arc segment's angular distance.

On a sphere or ellipsoid, the _____ is delineated along a great circle.

  a. Bounded
  b. Belt problem
  c. Best fit
  d. Central angle

18. _____ of Cyrene was a Greek mathematician, poet, athlete, geographer and astronomer. He made several discoveries and inventions including a system of latitude and longitude. He was the first Greek to calculate the circumference of the Earth , and the tilt of the earth's axis (also with remarkable accuracy); he may also have accurately calculated the distance from the earth to the sun and invented the leap day.
  a. Maria Gaetana Agnesi
  b. Archimedes
  c. Prime number
  d. Eratosthenes

Chapter 1. Measurement of Angles, Arcs, and Sectors 7

19. In physics, the _____ is a vector quantity (more precisely, a pseudovector) which specifies the angular speed of an object and the axis about which the object is rotating. The SI unit of _____ is radians per second, although it may be measured in other units such as degrees per second, revolutions per second, degrees per hour, etc. When measured in cycles or rotations per unit time (e.g. revolutions per minute), it is often called the rotational velocity and its magnitude the rotational speed.
   a. Amplitude
   b. Absolute value
   c. Additive identity
   d. Angular velocity

20. In physics, _____ is rotation along a circle: a circular path or a circular orbit. It can be uniform, that is, with constant angular rate of rotation, or non-uniform, that is, with a changing rate of rotation. The rotation around a fixed axis of a three-dimensional body involves _____ of its parts.
   a. Best fit
   b. Belt problem
   c. Bounded
   d. Circular motion

21. In physics, _____ is defined as the rate of change of position. It is a vector physical quantity; both speed and direction are required to define it. In the SI (metric) system, it is measured in meters per second: (m/s) or ms^{-1}.
   a. Belt problem
   b. Bounded
   c. Best fit
   d. Velocity

1. The _____ csc(A) is the reciprocal of sin(A), i.e. the ratio of the length of the hypotenuse to the length of the opposite side:

$$\csc A = \frac{\text{hypotenuse}}{\text{opposite}} = \frac{h}{a}.$$

The secant sec(A) is the reciprocal of cos(A), i.e. the ratio of the length of the hypotenuse to the length of the adjacent side:

$$\sec A = \frac{\text{hypotenuse}}{\text{adjacent}} = \frac{h}{b}.$$

The cotangent cot(A) is the reciprocal of tan(A), i.e. the ratio of the length of the adjacent side to the length of the opposite side:

$$\cot A = \frac{\text{adjacent}}{\text{opposite}} = \frac{b}{a}.$$

Equivalent to the right-triangle definitions the trigonometric functions can be defined in terms of the rise, run, and slope of a line segment relative to some horizontal line. The slope is commonly taught as 'rise over run' or rise/run. The three main trigonometric functions are commonly taught in the order sine, cosine, tangent.

   a. Belt problem
   b. Bounded
   c. Cosecant
   d. Best fit

2. The _____ of an angle is the ratio of the length of the adjacent side to the length of the hypotenuse. In our case

$$\cos A = \frac{\text{adjacent}}{\text{hypotenuse}} = \frac{b}{h}.$$

The tangent of an angle is the ratio of the length of the opposite side to the length of the adjacent side. In our case

$$\tan A = \frac{\text{opposite}}{\text{adjacent}} = \frac{a}{b}.$$

The remaining three functions are best defined using the above three functions.

a. Bounded
b. Cosine
c. Belt problem
d. Best fit

3. The _____ cot(A) is the reciprocal of tan(A), i.e. the ratio of the length of the adjacent side to the length of the opposite side:

$$\cot A = \frac{\text{adjacent}}{\text{opposite}} = \frac{b}{a}.$$

Equivalent to the right-triangle definitions the trigonometric functions can be defined in terms of the rise, run, and slope of a line segment relative to some horizontal line. The slope is commonly taught as 'rise over run' or rise/run. The three main trigonometric functions are commonly taught in the order sine, cosine, tangent.

a. Cotangent
b. Best fit
c. Bounded
d. Belt problem

4. The _____ of an angle is the ratio of the length of the opposite side to the length of the hypotenuse. In our case

$$\sin A = \frac{\text{opposite}}{\text{hypotenuse}} = \frac{a}{h}.$$

Note that this ratio does not depend on size of the particular right triangle chosen, as long as it contains the angle A, since all such triangles are similar.

The cosine of an angle is the ratio of the length of the adjacent side to the length of the hypotenuse.

a. Belt problem
b. Sine
c. Bounded
d. Best fit

Chapter 2. The Trigonometric Functions

5. In geometry, the _____ line (or simply the _____) to a curve at a given point is the straight line that 'just touches' the curve at that point (in the sense explained more precisely below.) As it passes through the point of tangency, the _____ line is 'going in the same direction' as the curve, and in this sense it is the best straight-line approximation to the curve at that point. The same definition applies to space curves and curves in n-dimensional Euclidean space.
   a. Best fit
   b. Belt problem
   c. Bounded
   d. Tangent

6. Trigonometry is a branch of mathematics that deals with triangles, particularly those plane triangles in which one angle has 90 degrees (right triangles.) Trigonometry deals with relationships between the sides and the angles of triangles and with the _____ functions, which describe those relationships.

Trigonometry has applications in both pure mathematics and in applied mathematics, where it is essential in many branches of science and technology.

   a. Best fit
   b. Belt problem
   c. Bounded
   d. Trigonometric

7. In mathematics, the _____ are functions of an angle. They are used to relate the angles of a triangle to the lengths of the sides of a triangle. _____ are important in the study of triangles and modeling periodic phenomena, among many other applications.
   a. Law of tangents
   b. Law of sines
   c. Trigonometric functions
   d. Law of cosines

8. The mathematical concept of a _____ expresses the intuitive idea that one quantity completely determines another quantity A _____ associates a unique value for each input of a specified type. The argument and value may be real numbers, but they can also be elements from any given sets: the domain and codomain of the _____.
   a. Best fit
   b. Function
   c. Bounded
   d. Belt problem

Chapter 2. The Trigonometric Functions 11

9. _____ is a part of mathematics concerned with questions of size, shape, and relative position of figures and with properties of space. _____ is one of the oldest sciences. Initially a body of practical knowledge concerning lengths, areas, and volumes, in the third century BC _____ was put into an axiomatic form by Euclid, whose treatment--Euclidean _____--set a standard for many centuries to follow.
   a. Bounded
   b. Belt problem
   c. Geometry
   d. Best fit

10. Two geometrical objects are called _____ if they both have the same shape. Equivalently and more precisely, one is congruent to the result of a uniform scaling (enlarging or shrinking) of the other. Corresponding sides of _____ polygons are in proportion, and corresponding angles of _____ polygons have the same measure.
   a. Similar
   b. Bounded
   c. Belt problem
   d. Best fit

11. A _____ is one of the basic shapes of geometry: a polygon with three corners or vertices and three sides or edges which are line segments. A _____ with vertices A, B, and C is denoted ABC.

In Euclidean geometry any three non-collinear points determine a unique _____ and a unique plane (i.e. a two-dimensional Euclidean space.)

   a. Best fit
   b. Bounded
   c. Belt problem
   d. Triangle

12. In mathematics, the _____ or Pythagoras' theorem is a relation in Euclidean geometry among the three sides of a right triangle . It states:

In any right triangle, the area of the square whose side is the hypotenuse (the side opposite the right angle) is equal to the sum of the areas of the squares whose sides are the two legs (the two sides that meet at a right angle.)

The theorem can be written as an equation:

$$a^2 + b^2 = c^2$$

Chapter 2. The Trigonometric Functions

where c represents the length of the hypotenuse, and a and b represent the lengths of the other two sides.

   a. Belt problem
   b. Pythagorean Theorem
   c. Bounded
   d. Best fit

13. In geometry and trigonometry, an _____ is the figure formed by two rays sharing a common endpoint, called the vertex of the _____ . The magnitude of the _____ is the 'amount of rotation' that separates the two rays, and can be measured by considering the length of circular arc swept out when one ray is rotated about the vertex to coincide with the other Where there is no possibility of confusion, the term '_____' is used interchangeably for both the geometric configuration itself and for its angular magnitude (which is simply a numerical quantity.)
   a. Absolute value
   b. Angle
   c. Affinely extended real number system
   d. Additive identity

14. A _____ is the longest side of a right triangle, the side opposite the right angle. The length of the _____ of a right triangle can be found using the Pythagorean theorem, which states that the square of the length of the _____ equals the sum of the squares of the lengths of the other two sides.

For example, if one of the other sides has a length of 3 meters (when squared, 9 m^2) and the other has a length of 4 m (when squared, 16 m^2.)

   a. Bounded
   b. Best fit
   c. Belt problem
   d. Hypotenuse

15. A _____ or right-angled triangle is a triangle in which one angle is a right angle (that is, a 90 degree angle.)

The side opposite the right angle is called the hypotenuse (side [BC] in the figure above.) The sides adjacent to the right angle are called legs or catheti (singular: cathetus.)

a. Belt problem
b. Right triangle
c. Bounded
d. Best fit

16. In geometry, an _____ is a triangle in which all three sides are equal. In traditional or Euclidean geometry, _____s are also equiangular; that is, all three internal angles are also congruent to each other and are each 60°. They are regular polygons, and can therefore also be referred to as regular triangles.
   a. Absolute value
   b. Isosceles triangle
   c. Additive identity
   d. Equilateral triangle

17. In probability theory and statistics, a _____ is described as the number separating the higher half of a sample, a population from the lower half. The _____ of a finite list of numbers can be found by arranging all the observations from lowest value to highest value and picking the middle one. If there is an even number of observations, the _____ is not unique, so one often takes the mean of the two middle values.
   a. Best fit
   b. Belt problem
   c. Bounded
   d. Median

18. In mathematics, the _____ or cyclometric functions are the so-called inverse functions of the trigonometric functions, though they do not meet the official definition for inverse functions as their ranges are subsets of the domains of the original functions. The principal inverses are listed in the following table.

If x is allowed to be a complex number, then the range of y applies only to its real part.

   a. Exsecant
   b. Exact constant expressions for trigonometric expressions
   c. Angle excess
   d. Inverse trigonometric functions

19. _____ are formed when a given transversal line crosses two coplanar lines. The _____ are not necessarily congruent. In the event that the _____ are congruent, these angles can be used to determine the degrees of the other angles of the parallel lines.

a. Belt problem
b. Bounded
c. Corresponding angles
d. Best fit

20. In combinatorial mathematics, given a collection C of sets, a _____ is a set containing exactly one element from each member of the collection: it is a section of the quotient map induced by the collection. If the original sets are not disjoint, there are several different definitions. One variation is that there is a bijection f from the _____ to C such that x is an element of f(x) for each x in the _____.
a. Bounded
b. Best fit
c. Belt problem
d. Transversal

21. In geometry, an _____ is an angle formed by two sides of a simple polygon that share an endpoint in. This angle must be an angle on the inner side of the polygon to be an internal angle. A simple polygon has exactly one internal angle per vertex.
a. Affinely extended real number system
b. Additive identity
c. Interior Angle
d. Absolute value

22. In Euclidean geometry, a _____ is a straight curve. When geometry is used to model the real world, _____s are used to represent straight objects with negligible width and height. _____s are an idealisation of such objects and have no width or height at all and are usually considered to be infinitely long.
a. Bounded
b. Best fit
c. Belt problem
d. Line

23. _____ is a branch of mathematics that deals with triangles, particularly those plane triangles in which one angle has 90 degrees (right triangles.) _____ deals with relationships between the sides and the angles of triangles and with the trigonometric functions, which describe those relationships.

_____ has applications in both pure mathematics and in applied mathematics, where it is essential in many branches of science and technology.

Chapter 2. The Trigonometric Functions

a. Bounded
b. Belt problem
c. Trigonometry
d. Best fit

24. A _____ is an instrument generally used to measure the altitude of a celestial object above the horizon. Making this measurement is known as sighting the object, shooting the object, or taking a sight. The angle, and the time when it was measured, can be used to calculate a position line on a nautical or aeronautical chart.

a. Best fit
b. Belt problem
c. Bounded
d. Sextant

25. The _____ of a geographic location is its height above a fixed reference point, often the mean sea level. _____, or geometric height, is mainly used when referring to points on the Earth's surface, while altitude or geopotential height is used for points above the surface, such as an aircraft in flight or a spacecraft in orbit.

Less commonly, _____ is measured using the center of the Earth as the reference point.

a. Affinely extended real number system
b. Elevation
c. Absolute value
d. Additive identity

26. In mathematics, a _____ is a circle with a unit radius, i.e., a circle whose radius is 1. Frequently, especially in trigonometry, 'the' _____ is the circle of radius 1 centered at the origin (0, 0) in the Cartesian coordinate system in the Euclidean plane. The _____ is often denoted S^1; the generalization to higher dimensions is the unit sphere.

a. Absolute value
b. Additive identity
c. Affinely extended real number system
d. Unit circle

27. A _____ is a simple shape of Euclidean geometry consisting of those points in a plane which are the same distance from a given point called the centre. The common distance of the points of a _____ from its center is called its radius.

_____s are simple closed curves which divide the plane into two regions, an interior and an exterior.

a. Circle
b. Belt problem
c. Bounded
d. Best fit

28. _____ generally conveys two primary meanings. The first is an imprecise sense of harmonious or aesthetically pleasing proportionality and balance; such that it reflects beauty or perfection. The second meaning is a precise and well-defined concept of balance or 'patterned self-similarity' that can be demonstrated or proved according to the rules of a formal system: by geometry, through physics or otherwise.
a. Bounded
b. Best fit
c. Belt problem
d. Symmetry

Chapter 3. Graphs of the Trigonometric Functions

1. The _____ of an angle is the ratio of the length of the adjacent side to the length of the hypotenuse. In our case

$$\cos A = \frac{\text{adjacent}}{\text{hypotenuse}} = \frac{b}{h}.$$

The tangent of an angle is the ratio of the length of the opposite side to the length of the adjacent side. In our case

$$\tan A = \frac{\text{opposite}}{\text{adjacent}} = \frac{a}{b}.$$

The remaining three functions are best defined using the above three functions.

a. Belt problem
b. Bounded
c. Cosine
d. Best fit

2. The _____ cot(A) is the reciprocal of tan(A), i.e. the ratio of the length of the adjacent side to the length of the opposite side:

$$\cot A = \frac{\text{adjacent}}{\text{opposite}} = \frac{b}{a}.$$

Equivalent to the right-triangle definitions the trigonometric functions can be defined in terms of the rise, run, and slope of a line segment relative to some horizontal line. The slope is commonly taught as 'rise over run' or rise/run. The three main trigonometric functions are commonly taught in the order sine, cosine, tangent.

a. Best fit
b. Belt problem
c. Bounded
d. Cotangent

3. The mathematical concept of a _____ expresses the intuitive idea that one quantity completely determines another quantity A _____ associates a unique value for each input of a specified type. The argument and value may be real numbers, but they can also be elements from any given sets: the domain and codomain of the _____.

Chapter 3. Graphs of the Trigonometric Functions

   a. Best fit
   b. Belt problem
   c. Bounded
   d. Function

4. The _____ of an angle is the ratio of the length of the opposite side to the length of the hypotenuse. In our case

$$\sin A = \frac{\text{opposite}}{\text{hypotenuse}} = \frac{a}{h}.$$

Note that this ratio does not depend on size of the particular right triangle chosen, as long as it contains the angle A, since all such triangles are similar.

The cosine of an angle is the ratio of the length of the adjacent side to the length of the hypotenuse.

   a. Sine
   b. Best fit
   c. Bounded
   d. Belt problem

5. A _____ typically refers to a class of handheld calculators that are capable of plotting graphs, solving simultaneous equations, and performing numerous other tasks with variables. Most popular _____s are also programmable, allowing the user to create customized programs, typically for scientific/engineering and education applications. Due to their large displays intended for graphing, they can also accommodate several lines of text and calculations at a time.
   a. Bounded
   b. Best fit
   c. Belt problem
   d. Graphing calculator

6. In mathematics, a _____ is a function that repeats its values in regular intervals or periods. The most important examples are the trigonometric functions, which repeat over intervals of length 2π. _____s are used throughout science to describe oscillations, waves, and other phenomena that exhibit periodicity.
   a. Bounded
   b. Periodic function
   c. Belt problem
   d. Best fit

Chapter 3. Graphs of the Trigonometric Functions

7. _____ is the magnitude of change in the oscillating variable, with each oscillation, within an oscillating system. For instance, sound waves are oscillations in atmospheric pressure and their _____s are proportional to the change in pressure during one oscillation. If the variable undergoes regular oscillations, and a graph of the system is drawn with the oscillating variable as the vertical axis and time as the horizontal axis, the _____ is visually represented by the vertical distance between the extrema of the curve.
   a. Amplitude
   b. Angular velocity
   c. Absolute value
   d. Additive identity

8. _____ is the number of occurrences of a repeating event per unit time. It is also referred to as temporal _____. The period is the duration of one cycle in a repeating event, so the period is the reciprocal of the _____.
   a. Belt problem
   b. Frequency
   c. Bounded
   d. Best fit

9. _____ is the motion of a simple harmonic oscillator, a motion that is neither driven nor damped. The motion is periodic - as it repeats itself at standard intervals in a specific manner - and sinusoidal, with constant amplitude; the acceleration of a body executing _____ is directly proportional to the displacement of the body from the equilibrium position and is always directed towards the equilibrium position.

The motion is characterized by its amplitude (which is always positive), its period, the time for a single oscillation, its frequency, the reciprocal of the period (i.e. the number of cycles per unit time), and its phase, which determines the starting point on the sine wave.

   a. Best fit
   b. Bounded
   c. Belt problem
   d. Simple harmonic motion

10. The _____ is the fraction of a complete cycle corresponding to an offset in the displacement from a specified reference point at time t = 0. Phase is a frequency domain or Fourier transform domain concept, and as such, can be readily understood in terms of simple harmonic motion. The same concept applies to wave motion, viewed either at a point in space over an interval of time or across an interval of space at a moment in time.

a. Bounded
b. Phase of an oscillation or wave
c. Best fit
d. Belt problem

11. In geometry, the _____ line (or simply the _____) to a curve at a given point is the straight line that 'just touches' the curve at that point (in the sense explained more precisely below.) As it passes through the point of tangency, the _____ line is 'going in the same direction' as the curve, and in this sense it is the best straight-line approximation to the curve at that point. The same definition applies to space curves and curves in n-dimensional Euclidean space.
   a. Best fit
   b. Belt problem
   c. Bounded
   d. Tangent

12. Trigonometry is a branch of mathematics that deals with triangles, particularly those plane triangles in which one angle has 90 degrees (right triangles.) Trigonometry deals with relationships between the sides and the angles of triangles and with the _____ functions, which describe those relationships.

Trigonometry has applications in both pure mathematics and in applied mathematics, where it is essential in many branches of science and technology.

   a. Best fit
   b. Trigonometric
   c. Bounded
   d. Belt problem

13. In mathematics, the _____ are functions of an angle. They are used to relate the angles of a triangle to the lengths of the sides of a triangle. _____ are important in the study of triangles and modeling periodic phenomena, among many other applications.
   a. Trigonometric functions
   b. Law of tangents
   c. Law of sines
   d. Law of cosines

14. In geometry, an _____ of a curve is a way of describing its behavior far away from the origin by comparing it to another curve. Specifically, the second curve is an _____ of the first if distance between the two approaches 0 as the points being considered tend to infinity. Informally, this means that the first curve gets closer to the second as it gets farther from the origin.

a. Affinely extended real number system
b. Asymptote
c. Additive identity
d. Absolute value

15. The _____ csc(A) is the reciprocal of sin(A), i.e. the ratio of the length of the hypotenuse to the length of the opposite side:

$$\csc A = \frac{\text{hypotenuse}}{\text{opposite}} = \frac{h}{a}.$$

The secant sec(A) is the reciprocal of cos(A), i.e. the ratio of the length of the hypotenuse to the length of the adjacent side:

$$\sec A = \frac{\text{hypotenuse}}{\text{adjacent}} = \frac{h}{b}.$$

The cotangent cot(A) is the reciprocal of tan(A), i.e. the ratio of the length of the adjacent side to the length of the opposite side:

$$\cot A = \frac{\text{adjacent}}{\text{opposite}} = \frac{b}{a}.$$

Equivalent to the right-triangle definitions the trigonometric functions can be defined in terms of the rise, run, and slope of a line segment relative to some horizontal line. The slope is commonly taught as 'rise over run' or rise/run. The three main trigonometric functions are commonly taught in the order sine, cosine, tangent.

a. Bounded
b. Cosecant
c. Belt problem
d. Best fit

Chapter 4. Inverse Trigonometric Functions

1. The terms '_____' and 'independent variable' are used in similar but subtly different ways in mathematics and statistics as part of the standard terminology in those subjects. They are used to distinguish between two types of quantities being considered, separating them into those available at the start of a process and those being created by it, where the latter (_____s) are dependent on the former (independent variables.)

The independent variable is typically the variable being manipulated or changed and the _____ is the observed result of the independent variable being manipulated.

   a. Bounded
   b. Best fit
   c. Belt problem
   d. Dependent variable

2. The terms 'dependent variable' and '_____' are used in similar but subtly different ways in mathematics and statistics as part of the standard terminology in those subjects. They are used to distinguish between two types of quantities being considered, separating them into those available at the start of a process and those being created by it, where the latter (dependent variables) are dependent on the former (_____s.)

The _____ is typically the variable being manipulated or changed and the dependent variable is the observed result of the _____ being manipulated.

   a. Additive identity
   b. Affinely extended real number system
   c. Absolute value
   d. Independent variable

3. A _____ typically refers to a class of handheld calculators that are capable of plotting graphs, solving simultaneous equations, and performing numerous other tasks with variables. Most popular _____s are also programmable, allowing the user to create customized programs, typically for scientific/engineering and education applications. Due to their large displays intended for graphing, they can also accommodate several lines of text and calculations at a time.
   a. Belt problem
   b. Best fit
   c. Graphing calculator
   d. Bounded

4. _____ is the number of occurrences of a repeating event per unit time. It is also referred to as temporal _____. The period is the duration of one cycle in a repeating event, so the period is the reciprocal of the _____.

a. Frequency
b. Belt problem
c. Best fit
d. Bounded

5. In Euclidean geometry, a _____ is a straight curve. When geometry is used to model the real world, _____s are used to represent straight objects with negligible width and height. _____s are an idealisation of such objects and have no width or height at all and are usually considered to be infinitely long.
   a. Bounded
   b. Belt problem
   c. Best fit
   d. Line

6. The _____ is a test to determine if a relation or its graph is a function or not. For a relation or graph to be a function, it can have at most a single y-value for each x-value. Thus, a vertical line drawn at any x-position on the graph of a function will intersect the graph at most once.
   a. Bounded
   b. Vertical line test
   c. Belt problem
   d. Best fit

7. An injective function is called an injection, and is also said to be a _____ function (not to be confused with _____ correspondence, i.e. a bijective function.)

A function f that is not injective is sometimes called many-to-one. (However, this terminology is also sometimes used to mean 'single-valued', i.e. each argument is mapped to at most one value.)

   a. Additive identity
   b. Absolute value
   c. One-to-one function
   d. One-to-one

8. Trigonometry is a branch of mathematics that deals with triangles, particularly those plane triangles in which one angle has 90 degrees (right triangles.) Trigonometry deals with relationships between the sides and the angles of triangles and with the _____ functions, which describe those relationships.

Trigonometry has applications in both pure mathematics and in applied mathematics, where it is essential in many branches of science and technology.

Chapter 4. Inverse Trigonometric Functions

   a. Best fit
   b. Belt problem
   c. Bounded
   d. Trigonometric

9. In mathematics, the _____ are functions of an angle. They are used to relate the angles of a triangle to the lengths of the sides of a triangle. _____ are important in the study of triangles and modeling periodic phenomena, among many other applications.
   a. Law of tangents
   b. Law of cosines
   c. Law of sines
   d. Trigonometric functions

10. The mathematical concept of a _____ expresses the intuitive idea that one quantity completely determines another quantity A _____ associates a unique value for each input of a specified type. The argument and value may be real numbers, but they can also be elements from any given sets: the domain and codomain of the _____.
    a. Belt problem
    b. Function
    c. Bounded
    d. Best fit

11. The _____ of an angle is the ratio of the length of the opposite side to the length of the hypotenuse. In our case

$$\sin A = \frac{\text{opposite}}{\text{hypotenuse}} = \frac{a}{h}.$$

Note that this ratio does not depend on size of the particular right triangle chosen, as long as it contains the angle A, since all such triangles are similar.

The cosine of an angle is the ratio of the length of the adjacent side to the length of the hypotenuse.

   a. Sine
   b. Belt problem
   c. Bounded
   d. Best fit

12. The _____ of an angle is the ratio of the length of the adjacent side to the length of the hypotenuse. In our case

Chapter 4. Inverse Trigonometric Functions 25

$$\cos A = \frac{\text{adjacent}}{\text{hypotenuse}} = \frac{b}{h}.$$

The tangent of an angle is the ratio of the length of the opposite side to the length of the adjacent side. In our case

$$\tan A = \frac{\text{opposite}}{\text{adjacent}} = \frac{a}{b}.$$

The remaining three functions are best defined using the above three functions.

   a. Belt problem
   b. Cosine
   c. Bounded
   d. Best fit

13. The _____ cot(A) is the reciprocal of tan(A), i.e. the ratio of the length of the adjacent side to the length of the opposite side:

$$\cot A = \frac{\text{adjacent}}{\text{opposite}} = \frac{b}{a}.$$

Equivalent to the right-triangle definitions the trigonometric functions can be defined in terms of the rise, run, and slope of a line segment relative to some horizontal line. The slope is commonly taught as 'rise over run' or rise/run. The three main trigonometric functions are commonly taught in the order sine, cosine, tangent.

   a. Belt problem
   b. Cotangent
   c. Best fit
   d. Bounded

14. In geometry, the _____ line (or simply the _____) to a curve at a given point is the straight line that 'just touches' the curve at that point (in the sense explained more precisely below.) As it passes through the point of tangency, the _____ line is 'going in the same direction' as the curve, and in this sense it is the best straight-line approximation to the curve at that point. The same definition applies to space curves and curves in n-dimensional Euclidean space.

Chapter 4. Inverse Trigonometric Functions

a. Bounded
b. Belt problem
c. Best fit
d. Tangent

15. In mathematics, the _____ or cyclometric functions are the so-called inverse functions of the trigonometric functions, though they do not meet the official definition for inverse functions as their ranges are subsets of the domains of the original functions. The principal inverses are listed in the following table.

If x is allowed to be a complex number, then the range of y applies only to its real part.

a. Exact constant expressions for trigonometric expressions
b. Exsecant
c. Angle excess
d. Inverse trigonometric functions

Chapter 5. Basic Trigonometric Identities 27

1. In mathematics, the term _____ has several different important meanings:

    - An _____ is an equality that remains true regardless of the values of any variables that appear within it, to distinguish it from an equality which is true under more particular conditions. For this, the 'triple bar' symbol ≡ is sometimes used. (However, this can be ambiguous since the same symbol can also be used with different meanings, for example for a congruence relation.)
    - In algebra, an _____ or _____ element of a set S with a binary operation Â· is an element e that, when combined with any element x of S, produces that same x. That is, eÂ·x = xÂ·e = x for all x in S.
        - The _____ function from a set S to itself, often denoted id or id_S, is the function such that id(x) = x for all x in S. This function serves as the _____ element in the set of all functions from S to itself with respect to function composition.
        - In linear algebra, the _____ matrix of size n is the n-by-n square matrix with ones on the main diagonal and zeros elsewhere. This matrix serves as the _____ with respect to matrix multiplication.

A common example of the first meaning is the trigonometric _____

$$\sin^2 \theta + \cos^2 \theta = 1$$

which is true for all complex values of θ (since the complex numbers $\mathbb{C}$ are the domain of sin and cos), as opposed to

$$\cos \theta = 1,$$

which is true only for some values of θ, not all. For example, the latter equation is true when $\theta = 0$, false when $\theta = 2$

The concepts of 'additive _____' and 'multiplicative _____' are central to the Peano axioms. The number 0 is the 'additive _____' for integers, real numbers, and complex numbers. For the real numbers, for all $a \in \mathbb{R}$,

$$0 + a = a,$$

$$a + 0 = a, \text{ and}$$

$$0 + 0 = 0.$$

Similarly, The number 1 is the 'multiplicative _____' for integers, real numbers, and complex numbers.

   a. Additive identity
   b. Affinely extended real number system
   c. Absolute value
   d. Identity

Chapter 5. Basic Trigonometric Identities

2. Trigonometry is a branch of mathematics that deals with triangles, particularly those plane triangles in which one angle has 90 degrees (right triangles.) Trigonometry deals with relationships between the sides and the angles of triangles and with the _____ functions, which describe those relationships.

Trigonometry has applications in both pure mathematics and in applied mathematics, where it is essential in many branches of science and technology.

   a. Best fit
   b. Trigonometric
   c. Bounded
   d. Belt problem

3. In mathematics, the _____ are functions of an angle. They are used to relate the angles of a triangle to the lengths of the sides of a triangle. _____ are important in the study of triangles and modeling periodic phenomena, among many other applications.
   a. Law of cosines
   b. Law of sines
   c. Law of tangents
   d. Trigonometric functions

4. The mathematical concept of a _____ expresses the intuitive idea that one quantity completely determines another quantity A _____ associates a unique value for each input of a specified type. The argument and value may be real numbers, but they can also be elements from any given sets: the domain and codomain of the _____.
   a. Bounded
   b. Function
   c. Belt problem
   d. Best fit

5. A _____ is an expression that compares quantities relative to each other. The most common examples involve two quantities, but any number of quantities can be compared. _____s are represented mathematically by separating each quantity with a colon, for example the _____ 2:3, which is read as the _____ 'two to three'.
   a. Belt problem
   b. Ratio
   c. Best fit
   d. Bounded

6. In geometry and trigonometry, an _____ is the figure formed by two rays sharing a common endpoint, called the vertex of the _____ . The magnitude of the _____ is the 'amount of rotation' that separates the two rays, and can be measured by considering the length of circular arc swept out when one ray is rotated about the vertex to coincide with the other Where there is no possibility of confusion, the term '_____' is used interchangeably for both the geometric configuration itself and for its angular magnitude (which is simply a numerical quantity.)

   a. Additive identity
   b. Absolute value
   c. Angle
   d. Affinely extended real number system

Chapter 6. Sum and Difference Identities

1. In mathematics, a function f is _____ of a function g if f(A) = g(B) whenever A and B are complementary angles. This definition typically applies to trigonometric functions.

For example, sine and cosine are _____s of each other (hence the 'co' in 'cosine'):

The same is true of secant and cosecant and of tangent and cotangent:

Sometimes writing a function in terms of its _____ helps solve trigonometric equations.

   a. Best fit
   b. Belt problem
   c. Bounded
   d. Cofunction

2. A pair of angles are complementary if the sum of their measures is 90 degrees.

If the two _____ are adjacent (i.e. have a common vertex and share just one side) their non-shared sides form a right angle.

In Euclidean geometry, the two acute angles in a right triangle are complementary, because the sum of internal angles of a triangle is 180 degrees, and the right angle itself accounts for ninety degrees.

   a. Best fit
   b. Complementary angles
   c. Belt problem
   d. Line

3. In geometry and trigonometry, an _____ is the figure formed by two rays sharing a common endpoint, called the vertex of the _____ . The magnitude of the _____ is the 'amount of rotation' that separates the two rays, and can be measured by considering the length of circular arc swept out when one ray is rotated about the vertex to coincide with the other Where there is no possibility of confusion, the term '_____' is used interchangeably for both the geometric configuration itself and for its angular magnitude (which is simply a numerical quantity.)
   a. Absolute value
   b. Affinely extended real number system
   c. Angle
   d. Additive identity

Chapter 6. Sum and Difference Identities 31

4. In mathematics, the term _____ has several different important meanings:

  - An _____ is an equality that remains true regardless of the values of any variables that appear within it, to distinguish it from an equality which is true under more particular conditions. For this, the 'triple bar' symbol ≡ is sometimes used. (However, this can be ambiguous since the same symbol can also be used with different meanings, for example for a congruence relation.)
  - In algebra, an _____ or _____ element of a set S with a binary operation Â· is an element e that, when combined with any element x of S, produces that same x. That is, eÂ·x = xÂ·e = x for all x in S.
    - The _____ function from a set S to itself, often denoted id or id_S, is the function such that id(x) = x for all x in S. This function serves as the _____ element in the set of all functions from S to itself with respect to function composition.
    - In linear algebra, the _____ matrix of size n is the n-by-n square matrix with ones on the main diagonal and zeros elsewhere. This matrix serves as the _____ with respect to matrix multiplication.

A common example of the first meaning is the trigonometric _____

$$\sin^2 \theta + \cos^2 \theta = 1$$

which is true for all complex values of θ (since the complex numbers $\mathbb{C}$ are the domain of sin and cos), as opposed to

$$\cos \theta = 1,$$

which is true only for some values of θ, not all. For example, the latter equation is true when $\theta = 0$, false when $\theta = 2$

The concepts of 'additive _____' and 'multiplicative _____' are central to the Peano axioms. The number 0 is the 'additive _____' for integers, real numbers, and complex numbers. For the real numbers, for all $a \in \mathbb{R}$,

$$0 + a = a,$$

$$a + 0 = a, \text{ and}$$

$$0 + 0 = 0.$$

Similarly, The number 1 is the 'multiplicative _____' for integers, real numbers, and complex numbers.

  a. Affinely extended real number system
  b. Absolute value
  c. Identity
  d. Additive identity

Chapter 7. Additional Identities

1. In mathematics, the term _____ has several different important meanings:

   - An _____ is an equality that remains true regardless of the values of any variables that appear within it, to distinguish it from an equality which is true under more particular conditions. For this, the 'triple bar' symbol ≡ is sometimes used. (However, this can be ambiguous since the same symbol can also be used with different meanings, for example for a congruence relation.)
   - In algebra, an _____ or _____ element of a set S with a binary operation Â· is an element e that, when combined with any element x of S, produces that same x. That is, eÂ·x = xÂ·e = x for all x in S.
     - The _____ function from a set S to itself, often denoted id or id_S, is the function such that id(x) = x for all x in S. This function serves as the _____ element in the set of all functions from S to itself with respect to function composition.
     - In linear algebra, the _____ matrix of size n is the n-by-n square matrix with ones on the main diagonal and zeros elsewhere. This matrix serves as the _____ with respect to matrix multiplication.

A common example of the first meaning is the trigonometric _____

$$\sin^2 \theta + \cos^2 \theta = 1$$

which is true for all complex values of θ (since the complex numbers $\mathbb{C}$ are the domain of sin and cos), as opposed to

$$\cos \theta = 1,$$

which is true only for some values of θ, not all. For example, the latter equation is true when $\theta = 0$, false when $\theta = 2$

The concepts of 'additive _____' and 'multiplicative _____' are central to the Peano axioms. The number 0 is the 'additive _____' for integers, real numbers, and complex numbers. For the real numbers, for all $a \in \mathbb{R}$,

$$0 + a = a,$$

$a + 0 = a$, and

$$0 + 0 = 0.$$

Similarly, The number 1 is the 'multiplicative _____' for integers, real numbers, and complex numbers.

a. Additive identity
b. Identity
c. Absolute value
d. Affinely extended real number system

Chapter 8. Trigonometric Equations

1. Trigonometry is a branch of mathematics that deals with triangles, particularly those plane triangles in which one angle has 90 degrees (right triangles.) Trigonometry deals with relationships between the sides and the angles of triangles and with the _____ functions, which describe those relationships.

Trigonometry has applications in both pure mathematics and in applied mathematics, where it is essential in many branches of science and technology.

   a. Trigonometric
   b. Bounded
   c. Belt problem
   d. Best fit

2. In mathematics, a _____ is a polynomial equation of the second degree. The general form is

$$ax^2 + bx + c = 0,$$

where x represents a variable, and a, b, and c, represent constants, with a ≠ 0. (If a = 0, the equation becomes a linear equation.)

   a. Belt problem
   b. Best fit
   c. Bounded
   d. Quadratic equation

3. The mathematical concept of a _____ expresses the intuitive idea that one quantity completely determines another quantity A _____ associates a unique value for each input of a specified type. The argument and value may be real numbers, but they can also be elements from any given sets: the domain and codomain of the _____.
   a. Best fit
   b. Belt problem
   c. Bounded
   d. Function

Chapter 8. Trigonometric Equations

4. In mathematics, the term _____ has several different important meanings:

- An _____ is an equality that remains true regardless of the values of any variables that appear within it, to distinguish it from an equality which is true under more particular conditions. For this, the 'triple bar' symbol ≡ is sometimes used. (However, this can be ambiguous since the same symbol can also be used with different meanings, for example for a congruence relation.)
- In algebra, an _____ or _____ element of a set S with a binary operation Â· is an element e that, when combined with any element x of S, produces that same x. That is, eÂ·x = xÂ·e = x for all x in S.
  - The _____ function from a set S to itself, often denoted id or id_S, is the function such that id(x) = x for all x in S. This function serves as the _____ element in the set of all functions from S to itself with respect to function composition.
  - In linear algebra, the _____ matrix of size n is the n-by-n square matrix with ones on the main diagonal and zeros elsewhere. This matrix serves as the _____ with respect to matrix multiplication.

A common example of the first meaning is the trigonometric _____

$$\sin^2 \theta + \cos^2 \theta = 1$$

which is true for all complex values of θ (since the complex numbers $\mathbb{C}$ are the domain of sin and cos), as opposed to

$$\cos \theta = 1,$$

which is true only for some values of θ, not all. For example, the latter equation is true when $\theta = 0$, false when $\theta = 2$

The concepts of 'additive _____' and 'multiplicative _____' are central to the Peano axioms. The number 0 is the 'additive _____' for integers, real numbers, and complex numbers. For the real numbers, for all $a \in \mathbb{R}$,

$$0 + a = a,$$

$$a + 0 = a, \text{ and}$$

$$0 + 0 = 0.$$

Similarly, The number 1 is the 'multiplicative _____' for integers, real numbers, and complex numbers.

a. Identity
b. Additive identity
c. Absolute value
d. Affinely extended real number system

Chapter 9. Law of Sines and Law of Cosines

1. The _____, in trigonometry, is a statement about any triangle in a plane, and an analogous statement in spherical trigonometry about triangles on a sphere. Where the sides of the triangle are a, b and c and the angles opposite those sides are A, B and C, then the _____ states that:

$$\frac{a}{\sin A} = \frac{b}{\sin B} = \frac{c}{\sin C}.$$

The common value of these three fractions is the diameter of the triangle's circumcircle. The _____ is also sometimes stated as

$$\frac{\sin A}{a} = \frac{\sin B}{b} = \frac{\sin C}{c}.$$

This law is useful when computing the remaining sides of a triangle if two angles and a side are known, a common problem in the technique of triangulation.

a. Proofs of trigonometric identities
b. Law of tangents
c. Law of cosines
d. Law of sines

2. The _____ of an angle is the ratio of the length of the opposite side to the length of the hypotenuse. In our case

$$\sin A = \frac{\text{opposite}}{\text{hypotenuse}} = \frac{a}{h}.$$

Note that this ratio does not depend on size of the particular right triangle chosen, as long as it contains the angle A, since all such triangles are similar.

The cosine of an angle is the ratio of the length of the adjacent side to the length of the hypotenuse.

a. Belt problem
b. Bounded
c. Best fit
d. Sine

3. In its simplest meaning in mathematics and logic, an _____ is an action or procedure which produces a new value from one or more input values. There are two common types of _____s: unary and binary. Unary _____s involve only one value, such as negation and trigonometric functions.

a. Operation
b. Affinely extended real number system
c. Absolute value
d. Additive identity

4. In mathematics and computer programming, when a number or expression is both preceded and followed by an operator such as minus or times, a rule is needed to specify which operator should be applied first; this rule is known as a _____, or more informally order of operation. From the earliest use of mathematical notation, multiplication took precedence over addition, whichever side of a number it appeared on. Thus 3 + 4 × 5 = 5 × 4 + 3 = 23.
a. Belt problem
b. Best fit
c. Precedence rule
d. Bounded

5. In trigonometry, the _____ is a statement about a general triangle which relates the lengths of its sides to the cosine of one of its angles. Using notation as in Fig. 1, the _____ states that

$$c^2 = a^2 + b^2 - 2ab\cos(\gamma),$$

or, equivalently:

$$b^2 = c^2 + a^2 - 2ca\cos(\beta),$$

$$a^2 = b^2 + c^2 - 2bc\cos(\alpha),$$

$$\cos(\gamma) = \frac{a^2 + b^2 - c^2}{2ab},$$

$$\cos(\beta) = \frac{a^2 + c^2 - b^2}{2ca},$$

$$\cos(\alpha) = \frac{b^2 + c^2 - a^2}{2bc}.$$

Note that c is the side opposite of angle γ, and that a and b are the two sides enclosing γ.

Chapter 9. Law of Sines and Law of Cosines

a. Proofs of trigonometric identities
b. Law of cosines
c. Law of tangents
d. Law of sines

6. The _____ of an angle is the ratio of the length of the adjacent side to the length of the hypotenuse. In our case

$$\cos A = \frac{\text{adjacent}}{\text{hypotenuse}} = \frac{b}{h}.$$

The tangent of an angle is the ratio of the length of the opposite side to the length of the adjacent side. In our case

$$\tan A = \frac{\text{opposite}}{\text{adjacent}} = \frac{a}{b}.$$

The remaining three functions are best defined using the above three functions.

a. Bounded
b. Belt problem
c. Best fit
d. Cosine

7. A _____ is one of the basic shapes of geometry: a polygon with three corners or vertices and three sides or edges which are line segments. A _____ with vertices A, B, and C is denoted ABC.

In Euclidean geometry any three non-collinear points determine a unique _____ and a unique plane (i.e. a two-dimensional Euclidean space.)

a. Bounded
b. Belt problem
c. Triangle
d. Best fit

8. In geometry, the _____ of a polygon is half its perimeter. Although it has such a simple derivation from the perimeter, the _____ appears frequently enough in formulas for triangles and other figures that it is given a separate name. When the _____ occurs as part of a formula, it is typically denoted by the letter s.

a. Belt problem
b. Best fit
c. Bounded
d. Semiperimeter

Chapter 10. Vectors

1. _____ as the name suggests is communication through graphics and graphical aids. It is the process of creating, producing, and distributing material incorporating words and images to convey data, concepts, and emotions.

   The field of _____s encompasses all phases of the _____s processes from origination of the idea (design, layout, and typography) through reproduction, finishing and distribution of two- or three-dimensional products or electronic transmissions.

   a. Best fit
   b. Belt problem
   c. Graphic communication
   d. Bounded

2. In mathematics, the _____ of two monic polynomials P and Q over a field k is defined as the product

$$\text{res}(P,Q) = \prod_{(x,y):\, P(x)=0,\, Q(y)=0} (x-y),$$

of the differences of their roots, where x and y take on values in the algebraic closure of k. For non-monic polynomials with leading coefficients p and q, respectively, the above product is multiplied by

$$p^{\deg Q} q^{\deg P}.$$

- The _____ is the determinant of the Sylvester matrix (and of the Bezout matrix.)

- When Q is separable, the above product can be rewritten to

$$\text{res}(P,Q) = \prod_{P(x)=0} Q(x)$$

  and this expression remains unchanged if Q is reduced modulo P. Note that, when non-monic, this includes the factor $q^{\deg P}$ but still needs the factor $p^{\deg Q}$.

- Let $P' = P \mod Q$. The above idea can be continued by swapping the roles of P' and Q. However, P' has a set of roots different from that of P. This can be resolved by writing $\prod_{Q(y)=0} P'(y)$ as a determinant again, where P' has leading zero coefficients. This determinant can now be simplified by iterative expansion with respect to the column, where only the leading coefficient q of Q appears.

$$\text{res}(P,Q) = q^{\deg P - \deg P'} \cdot \text{res}(P', Q)$$

Continuing this procedure ends up in a variant of the Euclidean algorithm. This procedure needs quadratic runtime.

a. Resultant
b. Belt problem
c. Bounded
d. Best fit

3. _____ is a part of mathematics concerned with questions of size, shape, and relative position of figures and with properties of space. _____ is one of the oldest sciences. Initially a body of practical knowledge concerning lengths, areas, and volumes, in the third century BC _____ was put into an axiomatic form by Euclid, whose treatment--Euclidean _____--set a standard for many centuries to follow.
a. Geometry
b. Best fit
c. Belt problem
d. Bounded

4. A _____ is one of the basic shapes of geometry: a polygon with three corners or vertices and three sides or edges which are line segments. A _____ with vertices A, B, and C is denoted ABC.

In Euclidean geometry any three non-collinear points determine a unique _____ and a unique plane (i.e. a two-dimensional Euclidean space.)

a. Triangle
b. Bounded
c. Best fit
d. Belt problem

5. In informal usage, _____ systems can have singularities: these are points where one or more of the _____s is not well-defined. For example, the origin in the polar _____ system (r,θ) on the plane is singular, because although the radial _____ has a well-defined value (r = 0) at the origin, θ can be any angle, and so is not a well-defined function at the origin. The Cartesian _____ system in the plane.

The prototypical example of a _____ system is the Cartesian _____ system, which describes the position of a point P in the Euclidean space R^n by an n-tuple

$$P = (r_1, ..., r_n)$$

of real numbers

$$r_1, ..., r_n.$$

Chapter 10. Vectors

a. Bounded
b. Best fit
c. Coordinate
d. Belt problem

6. In mathematics, a _____ in a normed vector space is a vector (often a spatial vector) whose length is 1 (the unit length.) A _____ is often denoted by a lowercase letter with a superscribed caret or 'hat', like this: $\hat{\imath}$.

In Euclidean space, the dot product of two _____s is simply the cosine of the angle between them.

a. Additive identity
b. Absolute value
c. Affinely extended real number system
d. Unit vector

7. In mathematics, the _____ is an operation which takes two vectors over the real numbers R and returns a real-valued scalar quantity. It is the standard inner product of the orthonormal Euclidean space. It contrasts with the cross product which produces a vector result.
a. Bounded
b. Dot product
c. Belt problem
d. Best fit

8. The _____ is one of the original six simple machines; as the name suggests, it is a flat surface whose endpoints are at different heights. By moving an object up an _____ rather than completely vertical, the amount of force required is reduced, at the expense of increasing the distance the object must travel. The mechanical advantage of an _____ is the ratio of the length of the sloped surface to the height it spans; this may also be expressed as the cosecant of the angle between the plane and the horizontal.
a. Additive identity
b. Affinely extended real number system
c. Absolute value
d. Inclined plane

9. In mathematics, two vectors are _____ if they are perpendicular, i.e., they form a right angle. The word comes from the Greek á½€ρθÏŒς , meaning 'straight', and γωνία (gonia), meaning 'angle'. For example, a subway and the street above, although they do not physically intersect, are _____ if they cross at a right angle.

a. Additive identity
b. Absolute value
c. Affinely extended real number system
d. Orthogonal

10. In geometry and trigonometry, an _____ is the figure formed by two rays sharing a common endpoint, called the vertex of the _____ . The magnitude of the _____ is the 'amount of rotation' that separates the two rays, and can be measured by considering the length of circular arc swept out when one ray is rotated about the vertex to coincide with the other Where there is no possibility of confusion, the term '_____' is used interchangeably for both the geometric configuration itself and for its angular magnitude (which is simply a numerical quantity.)
a. Affinely extended real number system
b. Angle
c. Absolute value
d. Additive identity

1. A _____, in mathematics, is a number comprising a real number part and an imaginary number part; it is normally written in the form a + bi, where a and b are real numbers, and i is the square root of minus one.

_____s are a field in mathematics, with specific notions of addition, subtraction, multiplication and division, satisfying certain axioms. These operations extend the corresponding operations on real numbers, mainly because the product of two imaginary numbers (or the square of one imaginary number) is a negative real number.

   a. Complex number
   b. Best fit
   c. Bounded
   d. Belt problem

2. An _____, in mathematics, is a number in the form bi where b is a real number and i is the square root of minus one, known as the imaginary unit. _____s and real numbers may be combined as complex numbers in the form a + bi where a is the real part and bi is the imaginary part. _____s can therefore be thought of as complex numbers where the real part is zero.
   a. Additive identity
   b. Affinely extended real number system
   c. Absolute value
   d. Imaginary number

3. In its simplest meaning in mathematics and logic, an _____ is an action or procedure which produces a new value from one or more input values. There are two common types of _____s: unary and binary. Unary _____s involve only one value, such as negation and trigonometric functions.
   a. Operation
   b. Additive identity
   c. Absolute value
   d. Affinely extended real number system

4. In mathematics, physics, and engineering, the _____ is denoted by i or the Latin j or the Greek iota . It allows the real number system, $\mathbb{R}$, to be extended to the complex number system, $\mathbb{C}$. Its precise definition is dependent upon the particular method of extension.

The primary motivation for this extension is the fact that not every polynomial equation with real coefficients f(x) = 0 has a solution in the real numbers.

Chapter 11. Complex Numbers

   a. Imaginary unit
   b. Imaginary part
   c. Additive identity
   d. Absolute value

5. _____ as the name suggests is communication through graphics and graphical aids. It is the process of creating, producing, and distributing material incorporating words and images to convey data, concepts, and emotions.

The field of _____s encompasses all phases of the _____s processes from origination of the idea (design, layout, and typography) through reproduction, finishing and distribution of two- or three-dimensional products or electronic transmissions.

   a. Best fit
   b. Belt problem
   c. Bounded
   d. Graphic communication

6. In mathematics, the _____ of a real number is its numerical value without regard to its sign. So, for example, 3 is the _____ of both 3 and −3.

The _____ of a number a is denoted by $|a|$.

   a. Absolute value
   b. Exponential Function
   c. Additive identity
   d. Absolute value

7. Alternatively to the cartesian representation z = x+iy, the complex number z can be specified by polar coordinates. The polar coordinates are r = $|z|$ ≥ 0, called the absolute value or modulus, and φ = arg(z), called the argument or the angle of z. The representation of a complex number by its polar coordinates is called the _____ of the complex number.
   a. Belt problem
   b. Bounded
   c. Best fit
   d. Polar form

8. Trigonometry is a branch of mathematics that deals with triangles, particularly those plane triangles in which one angle has 90 degrees (right triangles.) Trigonometry deals with relationships between the sides and the angles of triangles and with the _____ functions, which describe those relationships.

Trigonometry has applications in both pure mathematics and in applied mathematics, where it is essential in many branches of science and technology.

   a. Best fit
   b. Bounded
   c. Belt problem
   d. Trigonometric

9. In mathematics, a _____ is the result of a division. For example, when dividing 6 by 3, the _____ is 2, while 6 is called the dividend, and 3 the divisor. The _____ can also be expressed as the number of times the divisor divides into the dividend.
   a. Bounded
   b. Belt problem
   c. Best fit
   d. Quotient

Chapter 12. Polar Coordinates

1. In mathematics, the _____ system is a two-dimensional coordinate system in which each point on a plane is determined by a distance from a fixed point and an angle from a fixed direction.

The fixed point (analogous to the origin of a Cartesian system) is called the pole, and the ray from the pole with the fixed direction is the polar axis. The distance from the pole is called the radial coordinate or radius, and the angle is the angular coordinate, polar angle, or azimuth.

   a. Belt problem
   b. Polar coordinate
   c. Best fit
   d. Bounded

2. A position, location or _____ is a vector which represents the position of an object in space in relation to an arbitrary reference point. The concept applies to two- or three-dimensional space. The term is also used as a means of deriving displacement by the spatial comparison of two or more position vectors and are usually 2- or, through hyperspace-based theories, 3-dimensional or N-dimensional if belonging to an N-dimensional Euclidean hyperspace.
   a. Belt problem
   b. Best fit
   c. Bounded
   d. Radius vector

3. In informal usage, _____ systems can have singularities: these are points where one or more of the _____s is not well-defined. For example, the origin in the polar _____ system (r,θ) on the plane is singular, because although the radial _____ has a well-defined value (r = 0) at the origin, θ can be any angle, and so is not a well-defined function at the origin. The Cartesian _____ system in the plane.

The prototypical example of a _____ system is the Cartesian _____ system, which describes the position of a point P in the Euclidean space R^n by an n-tuple

$$P = (r_1, ..., r_n)$$

of real numbers

$$r_1, ..., r_n.$$

   a. Bounded
   b. Coordinate
   c. Belt problem
   d. Best fit

4. A _____ is closed curve with one cusp.

In geometry, the _____ is an epicycloid with one cusp.

Rolling circle around another fixed circle produces _____ Conformal mapping from circle to _____

- Epicycloid produced as the path (or locus) of a point on the circumference of a circle as that circle rolls around another fixed circle with the same radius.
- Limaçon with one cusp. The cusp is formed when the ratio of a to b in the equation is equal to one.
- An inverse curve of a parabola with focus as an inversion center.
- An image of circle $\partial D = \{w : abs(2w) = 1\}$ under complex map $w \to c = w - w^2$.
- Sinusoidal spiral : $r^n = a^n \cos(n\theta)$ for $n = \dfrac{1}{2}$

The name comes from the heart shape of the curve. Compared to the heart symbol (♥), though, a _____ only has one sharp point (or cusp.)

a. Cardioid
b. Belt problem
c. Bounded
d. Best fit

5. _____ generally conveys two primary meanings. The first is an imprecise sense of harmonious or aesthetically pleasing proportionality and balance; such that it reflects beauty or perfection. The second meaning is a precise and well-defined concept of balance or 'patterned self-similarity' that can be demonstrated or proved according to the rules of a formal system: by geometry, through physics or otherwise.
  a. Bounded
  b. Best fit
  c. Symmetry
  d. Belt problem

6. In mathematics, _____ are a method of defining a curve using parameters. A simple kinematical example is when one uses a time parameter to determine the position, velocity, and other information about a body in motion.

Abstractly, a relation is given in the form of an equation, and it is shown also to be the image of functions from items such as R^n.

a. Parametric equations
b. Bounded
c. Belt problem
d. Best fit

7. In Euclidean geometry, a _____ is a straight curve. When geometry is used to model the real world, _____s are used to represent straight objects with negligible width and height. _____s are an idealisation of such objects and have no width or height at all and are usually considered to be infinitely long.
   a. Best fit
   b. Belt problem
   c. Bounded
   d. Line

8. In mathematics, the _____ is an operation which takes two vectors over the real numbers R and returns a real-valued scalar quantity. It is the standard inner product of the orthonormal Euclidean space. It contrasts with the cross product which produces a vector result.
   a. Bounded
   b. Best fit
   c. Belt problem
   d. Dot product

ANSWER KEY

Chapter 1
1. b 2. b 3. b 4. b 5. b 6. d 7. a 8. c 9. c 10. b
11. b 12. b 13. d 14. b 15. d 16. d 17. d 18. d 19. d 20. d
21. d

Chapter 2
1. c 2. b 3. a 4. b 5. d 6. d 7. c 8. b 9. c 10. a
11. d 12. b 13. b 14. d 15. b 16. d 17. d 18. d 19. c 20. d
21. c 22. d 23. c 24. d 25. b 26. d 27. a 28. d

Chapter 3
1. c 2. d 3. d 4. a 5. d 6. b 7. a 8. b 9. d 10. b
11. d 12. b 13. a 14. b 15. b

Chapter 4
1. d 2. d 3. c 4. a 5. d 6. b 7. d 8. d 9. d 10. b
11. a 12. b 13. b 14. d 15. d

Chapter 5
1. d 2. b 3. d 4. b 5. b 6. c

Chapter 6
1. d 2. b 3. c 4. c

Chapter 7
1. b

Chapter 8
1. a 2. d 3. d 4. a

Chapter 9
1. d 2. d 3. a 4. c 5. b 6. d 7. c 8. d

Chapter 10
1. c 2. a 3. a 4. a 5. c 6. d 7. b 8. d 9. d 10. b

Chapter 11
1. a 2. d 3. a 4. a 5. d 6. d 7. d 8. d 9. d

Chapter 12
1. b 2. d 3. b 4. a 5. c 6. a 7. d 8. d

www.ingramcontent.com/pod-product-compliance
Lightning Source LLC
Chambersburg PA
CBHW081219230426
43666CB00015B/2812